James Douglas

Alison F. Gardner

Fitzhenry & Whiteside Limited

Contents

The Author

Alison Gardner lives in Vancouver. She has been a university librarian, researcher and adviser on international investment and, most recently, a writer for the B.C. Council of Forest Industries. She is now a freelance writer specializing in B.C.'s environment and history.

©1976, Fitzhenry & Whiteside Limited
150 Lesmill Road
Don Mills, Ontario, M3B 2T5

Printed and bound in Canada.

ISBN 0-88902-222-4

The Chapter 1
Mysterious
Lady

A small boy leaned against the rail of the sailing ship
gazing silently towards the shore. Beside him on the
deck stood a tall sunburned man, his hand resting on
the child's shoulder. A light breeze was blowing, but
it gave little relief from the tropical sun that beat
mercilessly down on their heads.

The boy's dark eyes were fixed on a young woman
standing absolutely still on the white sand a short
distance across the water. Only twenty minutes ago
she had kneeled down in the sand and hugged him
very hard. Her words still rang in his ears.

"Goodbye, James. Mind your father well and always
do as he advises." Her voice had broken a little as she
added, "Give my love to your brother when you see
him."

His mother and father had embraced only a
moment. Then his father extended a hand to the child
and quickly led the way to the waiting rowboat half
pulled up on the beach. A sailor had already loaded
their belongings into the front of the boat, and soon he
was stroking swiftly out into the little bay where they
would board the waiting ship.

Now the anchor was raised and one by one the sails
were set to catch the wind. The ship moved slowly
towards the mouth of the bay.

The waving figure on the beach grew smaller and
smaller, but still the child did not move. Finally his
father broke the silence, "We can go down now, son."

James Douglas never saw his mother again.

His father, John Douglas, was a wealthy Scottish
merchant whose family owned sugar plantations near

*James and his father probably
sailed to England in one of the
schooners used in the trade with
the West Indies. Many
schooners, like the Bluenose
shown on the Canadian ten-cent
piece, were built in Nova
Scotian shipyards.*

*How long did it take to sail from
the West Indies to Scotland in
the early 1800s? What were
conditions like on a sailing ship
in those days?*

Can you find Demerara on a map? The name of the country in which it is located has been changed since John Douglas's time. What is its name now? When and why was the name changed?

Demerara in British Guiana. From the time he was a young man, he had often travelled to the West Indies to inspect the plantations, and that is probably where he met James's mother. Although he never married her, he took full responsibility for the two sons and a daughter she gave him. As soon as the boys were old enough, he took them to Scotland to join his family there and receive a suitable education at schools in Scotland and later in England.

Where was James Douglas born? Who was his mother? In most people's lives, such questions are simple to answer. But with James Douglas, these basic facts remain a mystery. We know he was born in the year 1803, but that is all.

On most sugar plantations in the West Indies, black and mulatto servants or slaves were used to harvest the crops and make the sugar and molasses. James Douglas's mother was probably a mulatto servant on his father's plantation. What does "mulatto" mean?

Only he knew the story of his birth and, to the end of his life, he chose never to discuss the matter with anyone, not even his own family.

Distant Horizons Chapter 2

For the second time in his life, James Douglas stood at the rail of a sailing ship as it pulled away from the shore. But this time he was restless to gain the open sea for the seven-week voyage from Liverpool, England to the city of Quebec.

Ever since his brother, Alexander, had announced that he was going to North America to join the fur trade, James had been growing more and more impatient with his studies. Now, almost a year later, John Douglas had given his permission for his second son to follow the same path.

When he went ashore in Quebec on a clear June morning in 1819, James set out immediately for Montreal to receive instructions from his new employer, the North West Company.

The spring brigade preparing to leave Lachine, near Montreal for the journey West.

*A fur trade canoe on the
Mattawa River*

"En Route to the Trading Post"

As he was ushered into the company manager's office, the man looked him up and down. James was quite an impressive figure for a boy of sixteen. Already he was taller than most adults, and strong and well-built. The manager smiled approvingly and said, "You'll be going into tough country, lad, but then fur trading is a tough business as you'll soon find out. Just keep your head about you and you'll do very nicely, I've no doubt."

The next day James set out with a large party of Nor'Westers. He was assigned to one of the huge freight canoes, twelve metres long and two metres

Find out what you can about the life of the voyageurs *who worked for the fur trading companies.*
What are some of the best known voyageur *songs? Why did they usually have a very definite rhythm to them?*

wide. The frame was made of cedar covered with birch bark to make it as light as possible.

Paddled by sturdy French-Canadian *voyageurs*, the canoe carried the party further and further into the Western wilderness bound for the company's main fur depot at Fort William. From time to time, they were forced to make a portage around treacherous rapids. But even in calm waters, there was always the danger of striking a hidden rock or a dead tree and damaging the canoe.

James was fascinated by the hard-working *voyageurs* dressed in their gay coloured shirts and sashes. Most of them were small men with brown, weather-beaten faces, but in spite of their size, their strength was almost superhuman. Paddling the big canoe at such a pace was incredibly hard work, but the size of the packs they loaded on their backs for the portages was even more impressive.

Whenever the canoe reached open water and the crew could pick up speed, James urged them to sing. He loved the strong rhythm of their music and the colourful tales told in the songs. The hours passed quickly then and the loneliness of the silent land was forgotten for a time.

The party arrived at Fort William at the beginning of August. Immediately James set about learning the fur trade business, and one year later he was ready to be transferred to Ile-à-la-Crosse in what is now northern Saskatchewan. As a clerk, his salary for the next five years was set at £15 per annum.

At the Ile-à-la-Crosse trading post James came face to face with the bitter struggle going on between his company and its powerful rival, the Hudson's Bay Company. Competition was so fierce for the furs of the Cree and Chipewyan Indians who hunted in the area that violent clashes between the traders had become commonplace.

Tempers at the post were very short by the time James arrived there, and it wasn't long before he too got involved in the struggle. He soon developed a reputation for having a quick and violent temper which, on one occasion, ended in a duel with an equally hot-headed Hudson's Bay employee. Luckily no blood was spilled, but everyone agreed that young

Douglas was not a man to provoke.

James had been a clerk at Ile-à-la-Crosse for almost a year when bad news came from his company's headquarters in Montreal. The hated rival had won the fur trade war! The Hudson's Bay Company was about to take over all operations of the North West Company, including its employees if they wanted to stay on.

Why was the Hudson's Bay Company able to overcome the North West Company?

James had to make a difficult decision: he would either have to transfer his loyalties to the new company or leave the fur trade altogether. Like most of the North West Company's other employees, he eventually made up his mind to try working for the new company. He could never have guessed then that he would become a loyal servant of the Hudson's Bay Company for thirty-seven years!

After five years in the lonely outpost of Ile-à-la-Crosse, James was moved further west to New Caledonia, a vast territory covering most of the mainland of present-day British Columbia. He was twenty-two when he crossed the Rocky Mountains and for the first time set foot in the land that would be linked forever with his name. He would not leave it again until he was sixty-one years old. By then it would be a very different country, and he would be the man who helped to make it so.

Read up on the fur trade war between the North West Company and the Hudson's Bay Company. How were the two companies different in their operations and the way they treated their employees?

Chapter 3 **Fort St. James**

James arrived at Fort St. James just in time for a celebration. Kwah, the chief of the local Carrier Indians, had declared a two-day feast which the men at the fort were expected to attend.

Even though the Carrier village was some distance away, the sound of drums and chanting carried clearly over the lake to the fort. The music had been going on all morning when Peter, another of the company's clerks, poked his head in the door and said, "Aren't you coming, James? Old Kwah will be insulted if we don't show up soon!"

James recognized some of the Indian dishes from his years at Ile-à-la-Crosse. Roast beaver was one of his favourite meats, and bear he had tasted once or twice before. But some of the delicacies he did not know at all. He decided to ask Peter what they were before he tried them.

"What are those berries," he asked, pointing to a

The Indians near Fort St. James were called Carriers by the white traders because of a custom practised by the women of the tribe. When a woman's husband died, she carried his partly cremated remains in a small satchel on her back for several years before they were finally buried. Is there any other group of people who have a similar custom?

Fort St. James as it stood in James Douglas's time

heap of purple and red berries glistening in the
sunlight.

Watching for James's reaction, Peter explained that
they were mixed with rancid salmon oil. "That one," he
went on, pointing to another rather strong-smelling
fish dish, "is fish roe dug up specially for the occasion.
It's been maturing underground for a year or more!"

After the first excitement of the Carrier feast, James
explored his new surroundings for several days before
settling into the same post routine he had known at
Ile-à-la-Crosse. Up at dawn each morning, inspection
and prayers under the watchful eye of the fort's Chief
Factor, William Connolly, then assignment of his duties
for the day. One day it would be supervising repairs to
the freight canoes and sledges; another it might be
exchanging trade goods for furs with the Indians who
came to the post store.

Connolly soon noticed the newcomer who had

The trading store

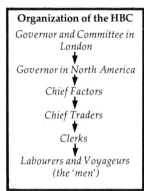

Organization of the HBC

Governor and Committee in London

↓

Governor in North America

↓

Chief Factors

↓

Chief Traders

↓

Clerks

↓

Labourers and Voyageurs (the 'men')

The salmon caught in the Fort St. James area swim all the way up the Fraser River from the Pacific Ocean. Why do they make this long journey? How important is commercial salmon fishing in Canada today?

How would you set up a fishery at the entrance to a lake? When the salmon were caught by the Hudson's Bay men, how were they dried?

Beaver fur hats

The Paris beau (1815)

The D'Orsay (1820)

by now grown into a serious young man with a powerful physique and an impressive height of 193 cm. Encouraged by James's knowledge of the fur trade and his attention to every detail of the Company's affairs, the Chief Factor decided to make him responsible for constructing a fishery on a small lake not far from the fort.

"Food is a serious problem at northern posts like this one," he told James. "I'm sure you have already heard some of the stories of terrible starvation faced by the Indians and white traders in this area. All it takes is a poor salmon run or even a late one, and the fort's food supply will be in trouble again.

"If you do a good job of setting up and running this fishery, we should be able to catch and dry enough fish to carry us through the year to the next salmon run."

Every man at the fort had a standard allowance of four whole salmon a day for as long as the supply lasted. He washed down this monotonous meal with water. If you were a clerk or better in the Company ranks, you could count on a few extra luxuries such as a ration of tea and sugar and perhaps some bacon on special occasions. This diet had changed very little since the fort was established, except for the addition of a few vegetables from the small garden just outside the pallisade gates.

In the few hours each day that were not taken up with Company matters, James's greatest pleasures were reading and writing. He had brought across the Atlantic and the North American continent his precious library of forty-five volumes of the *British Classics*, a history of England, a French dictionary and textbooks in geography, arithmetic and grammar. He read these over and over again, and when he was fortunate enough to find other books at the outposts he visited, he soon devoured those as well.

Writing was something he could do well, but always wanted to do better. Observations on his surroundings, his travels and the behaviour and habits of the Indians he committed to paper, but he rarely stopped there. By the light of a single candle flickering in the clerks' dormitory, he would write and rewrite an essay until he was satisfied with the style of the writing as well as his observations and ideas.

Ever since he had arrived in New Caledonia, James had wanted to see the Pacific Coast. Finally he got his chance. In the late spring of 1826, he joined the Chief Factor and half the men from the fort on the annual journey to deliver a precious cargo of furs to Fort Vancouver.

What were the most valuable furs collected in the New Caledonia region? On the Coast? What kinds of goods were made from these furs? Where were they sold?

The loaded freight canoes moved swiftly down the Fraser River as far as Fort Alexandria. There the canoes were abandoned and the men formed a pack train with horses to carry the furs to Fort Kamloops and on over the main brigade trail down the Okanagan Valley to the Columbia River. From there the party took to the water once again for the last lap by river to Fort Vancouver.

It was a long, dangerous trip of five weeks and

Trace the fur cargo route which the party from Fort St. James followed to Fort Vancouver. What sort of scenery would they have passed along the way? What dangers were they likely to encounter?

nearly 1600 km, but James still found the time to make extensive notes at the end of each day's travel. During the long winter months back at Fort St. James, he would turn the notes into letters and essays to send to his family and friends.

Everyone had special duties to perform during the visit to Fort Vancouver, but there was still plenty of time to sit in the warm sun and exchange news with the men of the Coast. All too soon it was time to load up the trading goods and supplies for the next year and retrace the route back to the northern interior.

One evening on the return trip, the Chief Factor was alone with James leaning against a log in front of the dying embers of the cooking fire. All the men had turned in, and the night sounds seemed louder than usual in the blackness surrounding them. A sentry stood guard some distance away on the edge of the camp.

Neither man spoke for a long time; then Connolly's voice broke the silence.

"I'm afraid I must have a word with you, James, about that temper of yours." He continued to look at the fire and went on before James could protest.

Fort Vancouver, the Hudson's Bay Company's first post in the West, was a pleasant haven after the hard journey from Fort St. James.

"I am sure it is often justified, but I cannot have you upsetting the Indians unnecessarily," he paused, "or the men for that matter.

"We are so few here and the Indians are many,"

the older man went on, "without friendship and co-operation among ourselves and with the Indians the fur trade would not be able to survive." He rose and looked straight at the young clerk, "Enough said, I think. See you in the morning, James." The Chief Factor turned and strode off to his tent.

James stayed in front of the fire for a long time turning the Chief Factor's words over and over in his mind. How could he argue with them? Of course, Connolly was right. His patience did seem to be getting shorter these days, although his temper had never been easy to control even when he was a child in boarding school.

He would have to give the matter some serious thought. One day his survival might depend on it.

Chapter 4 **Confrontation**

In the light of the late afternoon sun, James bent forward over a rough wooden table preparing his daily report for the company records.

It was nearly four months since Chief Factor Connolly had called him into this same room off the fort's mess hall. He had announced that the next week he was leaving for Fort Vancouver with the furs, and had decided to put James in charge while he was away.

James was surprised, but pleased to have this chance to show his administrative skills. As he turned to go, Connolly called him back.

"There is one more thing, James," the Chief Factor said. "As you know, these trips are difficult and there is always a chance that I might not get back. In fact, I have received reports that two of the tribes on our route have been restive this spring." He paused.

"When you asked permission to marry my daughter, Amelia, six months ago, I advised you to wait until she was older." He paused again.

"She is just now turned sixteen which is still a bit young, but under the circumstances I would like to see Amelia settled before I go. I presume you are still agreeable?"

James was certainly still agreeable. He had resigned himself to waiting several years, but he was ready to marry within the week if it meant he could have the woman of his choice.

Now a whole summer had passed and he expected his new father-in-law back from the Coast any time.

"Today," he wrote in the Company journal, "we had a good catch at the fishery, having netted four hundred and twenty-seven salmon moving upstream to their spawning grounds . . . ."

Suddenly his train of thought was broken by shouts and scuffling noises outside the door. As he pushed back his chair and rose to investigate, the door crashed open against the wall and Chief Kwah stood before him.

The Chief's eyes flashed as he waved his dagger in

James Douglas and Amelia Connolly were married "according to the custom of the country," just as Amelia's mother and father had been before them. What does this mean? Why did they marry that way?

James's direction. The knife was well-known in the territory as a swift and sure killer in the hands of the powerful Indian leader.

James hesitated only a split second, then lunged for his musket lying in the middle of the table. Before he knew what was happening, three of Kwah's warriors were upon him, pinning his arms behind his back. He struggled violently as the Indians tied a rope securely around his chest and arms and forced him back into the chair.

All the Company men were soon rounded up and marched into the room, each one guarded by a warrior holding a knife at his captive's throat.

"How did they get into the fort?" James snapped at the man nearest to him.

"Jumped us as we were unloading the fish from the sledge, sir. The gate was open and . . . ."

"Never mind," James interrupted him. He knew how hopeless it would have been to fight under the circumstances, but now he would have to think quickly or they would all be dead.

He turned his attention back to the Chief. "How dare you come here like this and attack men of the Hudson's Bay Company!" he spat out the words in the Carrier tongue.

The Chief laughed and thrust the blade of his dagger towards James's face to emphasize what he said.

"You have insulted me and my people. You came into my village when only women and children and old men were there and you killed Tzoelnolle. For that you and all your friends will die!"

James's face was hot and his heart raced. He took a deep breath and fought for control of himself.

He spoke very slowly now. "Tzoelnolle had to die. You know he murdered two traders of the Hudson's Bay Company two years ago, and gave their bodies to the village dogs to eat. When I heard that he had returned last week and was hiding in the village, I went there with my men and did to him what he had done to the others."

Before the Chief could reply, his nephew snatched the dagger from his hand and dashed forward to hold it at James's throat.

"Shall I strike, uncle?" he cried, "shall I strike?"

Chief Kwah's dagger was said to be the first metal knife owned by an Indian in that part of the country. It became a symbol of chieftainship among the Carrier Indians and was passed from chief to chief until the Hudson's Bay Company put it in their museum in Winnipeg. Can you find out where it is today and how it got there?

The other warriors urged him on, shouting, "Kill him, kill them all!" but the shouting stopped short as two young women burst into the room.

Amelia gasped as she saw her husband helpless in the chair. In a split second she and Nancy Boucher, the wife of the fort interpreter, were in front of Kwah questioning him sharply. Both the women had Indian blood in their veins, and they sensed immediately that this confrontation could mean death for everyone at the fort.

But Kwah turned his back and would not listen. The women ran quickly to the storeroom and gathered up all the tobacco, cloth and blankets they could carry. They rushed back and threw everything on the floor in front of the Indians crying, "This is for you if you go away and leave us in peace!"

The warriors soon turned their attention to the goods spread all over the floor, but they still kept a close watch on their captives.

Kwah raised his hand for silence and spoke directly to James.

"Young trader. You live because I wish you to live. Tzoelnolle deserved to die, but you should not have killed him in the village the way you did. I accept payment for this insult to his family and my village."

He turned on his heel and signalled the others to follow him.

The company men gazed after the Indians in stunned silence for almost a minute and then burst into cheering. Soon they were all talking and joking nervously about the close call they had had.

Only James remained silent. As soon as he was free of his ropes, he slipped away from the excited gathering and walked slowly to the other end of the fort enclosure where he could be alone to think.

His impulsive order to hunt down Tzoelnolle had almost cost them their lives. He thanked God that Chief Kwah had not been as rash even though he pretended to be.

In this brief showdown, James had learned something about himself and about the Indian people. He would carry both lessons with him for the rest of his life.

Headstone of Chief Kwah

ᑐ ᑐᑕ·ᙚ ᐦᐁ·
ᐁᗷᗷᕁ

1755 ᐱᐧ ᐊᗷᐧ ᐱᐧᑐ ᙆᐧᐁ ᐧᐁᐧ
1840 ᐊᑐᐧ ᐱᐧ ᑕᐧ ᙆᐁᗊ

ᙚᐁᑐᙚ ᐧᑎ ᐣᑐᙆ ᐁᐧᐳ
ᑐᐁᐧᐁᐧ ᐁᐳᐧ ᐁ ᗷ ᑎ
ᑕᐧᐦᐁ ᑐ᙭ ᑐᑌᐧ ᐸᐧ
ᐁᐧ ᐁᗷ ᑕᑐᑐ ᐱᐧ ᐳ
ᑐᑕᑐᐧᑎ.

HERE LIE THE REMAINS
OF
GREAT CHIEF
KWAH
BORN ABOUT 1755
DIED SPRING OF 1840

He once had in his hands the life of
future Sir James Douglas, but was great
enough to refrain from taking it

Chapter 5 **Preparing for Leadership**

It was a bitterly cold and windy day in January 1830 when James Douglas received word of his transfer to the Company's Columbia Department headquarters at Fort Vancouver. He made arrangements for Amelia to follow him after she had given birth to their first child later in the spring. Then he set out immediately for the south.

Fort Vancouver was the capital for the West Coast fur trade, linked by sea to every corner of the globe. Built five years earlier on the north bank of the Columbia River, it must have seemed to the Douglas

family a wonderfully civilized settlement after the isolation and primitive conditions of New Caledonia.

Within the fort's stockade were offices, warehouses, workshops, a schoolhouse and chapel, living quarters for the staff and the Chief Factor's residence. The whole layout was spacious compared to Fort St. James, and some of the buildings were even painted.

It had always been against Company policy for a post to become deeply involved in farming operations, but Fort Vancouver was an exception. The rich silt washed down by the Columbia River was too fertile to ignore, especially when most of the Western posts were desperately short of food every year.

So Fort Vancouver became the food basket with fertile fields of wheat, oats and barley and rows of fruit trees stretching far beyond the stockade walls. Cattle, sheep and hogs grazed over the hillsides and grew fat on the rich grass.

But if the land around Fort Vancouver was tranquil

Fort Vancouver, the food basket of the Western posts

Crossing the bar at the entrance of the Columbia River was often a hazardous undertaking.

and hospitable, the water was not. Every ship's captain dreaded crossing the dangerous bar that guarded the entrance to the river. Ship after ship was lost in those turbulent waters, often taking with it the whole crew and a year's precious supplies from England.

As was the Company custom, the men dined in the mess hall, discussing business affairs and smoking a pipe after the meal while chatting with visiting traders and travellers. The women seldom left their own quarters and rarely met any visitors, but this did not worry the shy young Amelia who preferred the company of her husband and her growing family above all else. Over the years, she gave birth to ten of the Douglas's thirteen children in the little rooms of their private quarters at Fort Vancouver, but only eight of the children survived infancy.

The Chief Factor of the Columbia Department was Dr. John McLoughlin, a striking figure well over 180 cm tall with large blue eyes and a shock of white hair reaching to his shoulders. The "Great White-Headed Eagle," as the Indians called him, took an instant liking to James and soon made him chief accountant for the Columbia Department. The two men worked happily together for the next fifteen years.

James travelled long distances during those years, several times crossing the Rocky Mountains to present his department's accounts to senior officials of the Company gathered at York Factory on Hudson's Bay. On one of these journeys he received his commission as Chief Trader with an increase in salary to £400 a year— a far cry from the humble salary of £15 he had received when he first arrived at Fort St. James. But he would not have to wait so long for his final promotion.

In September 1840 after twenty-one years of service, he became a Chief Factor, the highest rank possible in the Hudson's Bay Company field operations. He was now entitled to wear the Chief Factor's striking uniform with its white shirt, collars to his ears, frock coat, velvet stock and straps to the bottom of his trousers, a black beaver hat, long cloak of Royal Stuart tartan with a scarlet or dark blue lining, and a soft Genoa velvet collar which was fastened with mosaic gold clasps and chain.

But Douglas had little time to think about his new titles or magnificent suit of clothes. After years of making difficult and dangerous journeys east and west, he now started on a new series north and south along the Pacific Coast.

"The Great White-Headed Eagle"

First he set out aboard the trusty Company vessel, *Beaver,* for the Russian post of Sitka where the Governor of the Russian American Company supervised that country's trading operations. There Douglas negotiated the transfer of Fort Stikine from Russian to British hands, then moved on to build the most northerly post of the Hudson's Bay Company at Fort Taku.

Why did the Russians agree to hand over Fort Stikine and some of their trading territory to the British?

The Mexicans took over California from the Spanish in 1825. When did California become American and under what circumstances?

Hardly had he returned from the northern mists when he was dispatched on another diplomatic mission. This time he headed south to Monterrey, California to buy breeding cattle from the Mexican government and negotiate for the safe passage of the cattle overland back to Fort Vancouver. He even joined thirty Hudson's Bay Company officers and men on the trail drive as far as San Francisco riding horseback through the beautiful and fertile California countryside.

Douglas was deeply impressed by what he saw and recorded his observations in his journals and letters to friends and relatives. But he did not think much of the Mexican people or their system of government. As he later wrote to a friend:

> There is no country that has more attractions than California. I would cheerfully become a citizen of that country provided that I could do so in company with a party of friends respectable from their numbers, and powerful enough to restrain oppression . . . . In fact, I could have obtained a handsome grant of land on a simple application; but my views are not yet fixed as to the future.

But his attraction to the sun-drenched lands of the south soon passed, and once more he turned all his attention and energy to the Pacific Northwest.

"Our Days Are Numbered" Chapter 6

At the beginning of the nineteenth century, there were four major sovereign powers interested in the Pacific Coast of North America: Britain, the United States, Russia and Spain. Gradually, through diplomatic negotiation, Russia agreed to restrict her activities to north of latitude 54° 40′, and Spain to south of latitude 42°, which the Mexicans also agreed to when they took over the Spanish territory.

This left the United States and Britain to occupy jointly the remaining territory until a definite agreement could be reached.

By the early 1840s the Hudson's Bay Company, representing the British interests in the area, could see the writing on the wall: American settlers and traders were flooding into the West and rumours were circulating in London and Washington that the 49th parallel would finally become the international boundary between the British and American territories. If that happened, Fort Vancouver would be lost.

George Simpson, the Governor of the Hudson's Bay Company in North America, ordered immediate construction of a new post on southern Vancouver Island. The obvious man to pick the site and supervise the building of the new depot was Chief Factor James Douglas.

On a crisp autumn morning in 1842, a group of half-naked Songhees Indians, faces smeared with fish blood, peered through the low bush at the "smoking tree" that had appeared offshore. It was the long, thin funnel of the *Beaver*.

Douglas and his party of surveyors examined many sites in the area before settling on the best place to build Fort Victoria. Finally, eliminating all but two sites, he weighed the advantages of each in his journal:

The Beaver *had a long and interesting career on the Pacific Coast from its arrival in 1836 until it was wrecked off Vancouver in 1888. Why was it such a famous ship?*

I am at a loss where to place the fort, as there are two positions possessing advantages, though of different kinds. Number one has a good view of the harbour, is open, clear ground only fifty yards from the beach; on the other hand, vessels drawing fourteen feet cannot come within a hundred and thirty feet of the shore. We will, therefore, either have to [boat cargo] off and on at a great destruction of boats and considerable loss of time or be put to the expense of forming a jettie at a great amount of labour.

Number two, on the other hand, will allow of vessels lying with their sides grazing on the rocks, which form a natural wharf where their cargo may be conveniently landed from the ship's yard, and in that respect would be exceedingly advantageous; but, on the other hand, an intervening point intercepts the view so that the mouth of the port cannot be seen from it, an objection of much weight in case of vessels entering and leaving port. Another disadvantage is that the shore is there covered by thick woods to the breadth of two hundred yards, so that we must either place the fort at that distance from the landing place or clear away the thickets, which would detain us very much in our building operations. I will think more on this subject before determining the point. . . .

James Douglas in the uniform of a Chief Factor with his party of surveyors marking the site for Fort Victoria.

The Songhees Indians were very friendly and offered to help in the construction of the fort. They were happy to receive a Hudson's Bay blanket in payment for every forty cedar pickets that they brought to the site. The pickets were about six and a half metres long and almost a metre in circumference.

Because it was expected that one day it would become the most important Company depot on the Pacific Coast, Fort Victoria was designed on a larger scale than usual. The fort formed a square, one hundred and forty-two metres long on each side enclosed with pickets six metres above the ground. The bastions stood diagonally at two corners of the square, forming an important part of the fort's defence system. Inside the stockade, the wooden buildings were put together

What makes a Hudson's Bay blanket different from other blankets? Why did the Indians prize them so highly as a trade item?

The ground plan for Fort Victoria

PLAN of FORT VICTORIA

E

Gate

Bastion

Employees Houses

Chief factor and
Mess Hall

Men's Quarters
and School

Warehouse

N

Warehouse

Men's
Quarters

S

Powder
Magazine

Warehouse

Blacksmith

General
Store

Bastion

W

Gate

using wooden pegs. In this part of the world, nails were still too expensive to use except for special purposes.

Leaving a small staff of men at the new fort, Douglas returned to his duties at Fort Vancouver. As expected, the Oregon Treaty was signed two years later in 1846 giving the Americans all territory south of the 49th parallel. The Hudson's Bay Company retained its posts in the south for some time, but its days there were numbered.

Dr. John McLoughlin retired as head of the Columbia Department soon after the treaty was signed, leaving Douglas as the most important representative of the Hudson's Bay Company on the Pacific Coast. Two years later the British government agreed to give the company exclusive interest to the 36,260 km² of Vancouver Island for an annual rent of seven shillings. Fort Victoria would be the headquarters for the new fur preserve.

When the British government gave the Hudson's Bay Company exclusive interests on Vancouver Island, what did they expect from the Company in return? Did they get it?

The time had come for James Douglas to move his family for the last time to the island he had described to friends six years before as "a perfect Eden."

The Beaver in Fort Victoria harbour in 1846

Chapter 7 Welcome To Fort Victoria

Amelia Douglas at about 35 with two of her daughters

"Are you comfortable, my dear?" the Chief Factor asked as he spread a light rug over his wife's knees. Amelia looked anything but comfortable wedged into the corner of the heavy wooden wagon loaded with the family's belongings, but she had learned from experience that this was the only way to avoid being jolted around on the rough roads. The two youngest Douglas children played quietly in the small area that had been left clear for them in the back of the wagon.

Trying not to notice the lines of apprehension on her face, James swung easily onto his big chestnut horse and rode past five other wagons loaded high with the Company's property. At the front of the convoy he could see his three older daughters waiting impatiently astride their horses for him to join them.

As James knew, Amelia had every reason to look apprehensive about the journey. It was only after it was over that he could joke about the move from Fort Vancouver to Fort Victoria in the spring of 1849.

How did the Sandwich Islands get their name? What are they called today? Why were there many Sandwich Islanders working for the Hudson's Bay Company on the Pacific Coast?

. . . my staff was composed of one Sandwich Islander with an invalid sailor who instead of helping me required to be waited on. With that numerous and respectable train I had to guard our collected treasures of the preceding winter and spring—say 636 lb. of gold-dust and twenty packs of otters, worth altogether about £30,000, a noble prize for a gang of thieves.

But luckily no gang of thieves attacked the party and at Fort Nisqually they all boarded a ship to cross the Strait of Juan de Fuca to their new home.

What were the duties of a governor in a Crown colony? Who is the Queen's representative in Canada today? Compare his duties with those of a governor in Douglas's time.

Now that Vancouver Island was the focus of British activity on the Coast, Her Majesty's government decided that it was time to appoint a colonial governor. His task would be to govern all colonists not working for the Hudson's Bay Company and see that their interests were protected. There was only one problem. Vancouver Island had only a handful of colonists to govern and they were entirely dependent upon the Company for their safety and well-being anyway.

The British government soon faced the fact that Vancouver Island's development as a Crown colony could not yet be separated from the influence of the Hudson's Bay Company. It turned to James Douglas as the most logical choice for governor.

But Douglas was not keen on the idea. He was already working long and exhausting hours as Chief Factor, and the new job would only rob him of the precious little time he did have to enjoy his family and friends. It was difficult enough to be a loyal and efficient servant to one gigantic empire, but *two* of them would be impossible. What would he do if they did not agree on some matter of policy? It had happened before. To Douglas, loyalty was the strongest virtue a man could possess and he did not want to put himself in a position where he had to choose between two masters. His loyalty to the Queen was unquestioned, but he had served the interests of the fur trade empire for nearly thirty years and that was a hard habit to break.

On the other hand, it would be a great honour to serve as governor too, and he did like the pomp and ceremony that accompanied the position. The Hudson's Bay Company was urging him to accept, so perhaps they understood the situation better than he did.

He decided to accept. In the fall of 1851 James Douglas became the Governor of the Crown colony of Vancouver Island.

James Douglas in the full uniform of the Governor of Vancouver Island

Chapter 8 **Growing Pains**

What route did a ship from England to Vancouver Island normally take in the 1850s? What kinds of accommodation were available on board ship? Which one did most of the passengers choose? Why?

It was hardly surprising that settlers did not come rushing to the new colony. The only way for colonists to get from England to Vancouver Island was by sea, aboard a Hudson's Bay supply ship. The living conditions during the six-month voyage were so bad that many children and old people died before they reached their destination. But that was not the only hardship travellers had to endure. A trip was rarely completed without an outbreak of smallpox or a death from scarlet fever or measles. Supplies of fresh water and food soon ran out and for long periods passengers had to live on cheese and ship biscuits full of weevils.

When the weary and dejected newcomers finally reached Fort Victoria, they could not expect to find any accommodation until they built it for themselves. Food and other goods from the Company store were very expensive and nearly always in short supply.

But Governor Douglas worked hard to make his little colony a pleasant place in which to live and work. Although he was deeply devoted to the Anglican Church he gave surprisingly strong support to people of any other religious denominations who wished to preach their beliefs on the Western frontier. During his time at Fort Vancouver, he had set up schools and encouraged all children in the area to attend them. Now on Vancouver Island he continued this tradition, but he did not stop there.

What would a school in the Crown colony look like inside? Did boys and girls go to school together? What subjects were taught?

Always remembering his own experience at the Company's isolated outposts, he set up a circulating library of "solid reading matter" to keep the employees suitably occupied and improve their education. As far as the Governor was concerned, there was no worse sin than idleness.

Douglas insisted that even a colony as small as his required a police force. He soon raised enough money for a ten-man militia to which he gave the ringing title of Victoria Voltigeurs. With half French-Canadian and half Indian blood flowing in their veins, these were

strong, colourful men with a gift for tracking matched
by no one else in the colony. Dressed in tasselled caps,
long sky-blue cloaks, buckskin trousers and broad
scarlet sashes with gunpowder horns swinging from
them, the Voltigeurs soon came to be well-known all
along the Coast.

The Island's 26,000 Indians were also a matter of
special concern to Douglas. In a report to his superiors
in London, he described them as "a highly interesting
people, hospitable and always grateful for acts of
kindness." The British government had issued orders
to stamp out the practice of slavery among the West
Coast tribes, but Douglas realized that ancient
institutions can never be eliminated overnight. The
practice did gradually disappear, but not before he had
bought the freedom of several young slaves to
demonstrate his own strong feelings on the subject.

Occasionally there were acts of violence, most often
between rival tribes, but sometimes against Company
employees or colonists. The Governor always moved
swiftly to punish the offender, but he was a good deal
more cautious now than he had been in his Fort St.
James days. He believed very strongly in the colony's
British laws, and he wanted the Indian people to
appreciate their value too. But the course of justice was
by no means straightforward in practice.

The waterfront at Fort Victoria in 1854

Early in November of 1852, a chill ran through the settlement when a shepherd from the Hudson's Bay farm at Christmas Hill was murdered only a few kilometres from the fort. The culprits were a brave from the Cowichan band and the son of a Nanaimo chief.

As soon as he heard of the murder, Douglas dispatched messengers to each tribe informing their chiefs of the crime and demanding the surrender of the accused. As he had feared, there was no response.

Knowing the dangers of the next step he must take, he put all his private affairs in order and saw to the marriage of his oldest daughter, Cecilia, before leaving Victoria.

With one hundred and thirty seamen borrowed from a Royal Navy ship which happened to be in the area and his trusty Voltigeurs, the Governor led his imposing fleet of two vessels up the coast as far as the mouth of the Cowichan River.

He sent a messenger to summon the Chief of the Cowichans, then went ashore. A small tent was pitched on the beach. Dressed in full uniform and looking very dignified, Douglas sat inside surrounded by presents for the tribe. The party did not have to wait long.

The Indians swept down the river in their war canoes all "hideously painted . . . whooping like demons and drumming on their canoes by turns with all their might." There among them sat the Cowichan brave whooping and drumming harder than any of them.

Never having seen anything like this before, most of the seamen were petrified. One young officer later recalled that there were "over 200 tall warriors, their height exaggerated with head plumes, faces terrifically painted with ochre, decked with loin-ropes of shells which met their deer-skin leggings and clattered with every movement." He was not the only one who wondered if he would live to tell the tale!

It took Douglas a long time to persuade the tribe to give up the man he wanted, but finally they agreed. Then the expedition proceeded further up the coast to Nanaimo. The chief's son had already escaped far into the woods by the time they arrived, but the Voltigeurs were able to track him down and return him to the ship.

The Governor insisted on holding a proper trial with

a jury selected from the ship's officers. Both prisoners admitted their guilt, so there could be only one verdict.

"They were sentenced to be hanged," he wrote, "and the execution took place in the presence of the whole tribe, the scene appearing to make a deep impression upon their minds."

Douglas was more relieved than anyone when this mission was over. Grateful that such incidents were a rare occurrence, he returned happily to the routine management of the Crown colony.

After seven years under his care, there were three schools, six sawmills, three flour mills and thirty-nine stores scattered along the east coast of Vancouver Island between Victoria and Nanaimo. Only one thousand white people lived in the whole colony and many of them were small children. Very soon all that would change.

Douglas used English law and the jury system to try the two Indians. How did the Indians treat crimes committed within their tribes?

Chapter 9 **Gold Fever**

From the time of the Fraser River gold rush on, paddle-wheel steamers became the standard means of transport along the Coast. How did they operate? What facilities did they have on board for the comfort of passengers?

The Douglas family was thanking the Reverend Mr. Cridge for his excellent sermon on the evils of drunkenness when a young man dressed in the Voltigeur uniform burst into the church. He quickly spotted the tall figure of the Governor and pushed through the crowd of worshippers to reach him.

"Excuse me, sir," he said urgently. "Can you come outside right away?"

Douglas looked at him in surprise.

"What is it, Williams?" he asked, a little impatient at the interruption in his Sunday routine.

"It's a boat in the harbour, sir," Williams tried to explain. "It's unloading hundreds and hundreds of people." He flung his arms wide to emphasize his point. "I think you should come and see for yourself!"

By this time Douglas could hear the commotion

outside. He excused himself to Mr. Cridge, promising to continue their discussion at the earliest opportunity, and strode quickly down the aisle beside the Voltigeur.

Perched on a hill sloping down to the harbour, the little church was an excellent spot from which to view the spectacle below. Most of the townspeople, fresh from the Sunday morning service, stood watching with fascination as a steady stream of men poured off the sidewheel steamer, *Commodore*, lashed to the dock. They wore red flannel shirts, knee boots and broad-brimmed hats, and carried rolled up blankets, miners' washpans and spades. Even from this distance, it was possible to see a long knife or a revolver hanging from nearly every belt.

As Douglas made his way through the crowd, he spotted another Voltigeur panting up the hill towards him. He did not wait for the man to catch his breath before questioning him anxiously.

"What's going on? Who are these people and what have they come for?"

The Voltigeur blurted out, "They are from San Francisco, sir. They've heard about the gold on the Mainland." He took a deep breath, "And they say thousands more miners are on their way!"

Douglas looked back towards the harbour and shook his head in disbelief.

"Are they all Americans?" was his next question. He had always been well aware that the neighbours to the south had more than a passing interest in the British possessions on the West Coast. Since becoming Governor, he had taken every possible action to discourage Americans from entering the colony even in small numbers, but now it looked as though his worst fears were about to come true.

"No sir, they're not all American," the Voltigeur shook his head. "As far as I can tell only about sixty men are real Americans and the same number are British or Canadian. The rest of this load are Germans, French and Italians who came to the West years ago for the California gold rush."

And now I have my own gold rush to deal with, Douglas thought.

It was April 25, 1858, and the Fraser River gold rush was on.

Fort Victoria at the beginning of the gold rush in 1858. Already there are two sidewheelers in the harbour and a tent city is growing up outside the fort.

The little colony was suddenly faced with problems it had never dreamed possible. Victoria, with its population of only a few hundred colonists, was in no position to absorb the thousands of miners who flooded in every month during the summer of 1858. The settlement soon became a tent city with open sewers flowing down the hillside, roads thick with mud and pitted with deep potholes, and serious shortages of food and supplies.

Twenty-five thousand miners passed through Victoria that first year. American steamship companies advertised the discovery of a new El Dorado to the north. They made a fortune by reducing fares from San Francisco to Victoria from $75 to $30 and then filling the vessels to three times capacity.

Most of the miners stopped at Victoria just long enough to pick up provisions and tools, pay a licence fee to the government of Vancouver Island and then find some means of transportation to the Fraser River gold fields. Douglas's dispatch of May 8, 1858 to the Colonial Secretary in London captured the frantic scene:

Boats, canoes, and every species of small craft are continually
employed in pouring their cargoes into Fraser's River, and it is
supposed that not less than one thousand whites are already at work,
and on the way to the gold districts.

Many accidents have happened in the dangerous rapids of the
river; a great number of canoes have been dashed to pieces, and their
cargoes swept away by the impetuous stream, while of the ill-fated
adventurers who accompanied them, many have been swept into
eternity.

The others, nothing daunted by the spectacle of ruin, and buoyed
up by the hope of amassing wealth, keep pressing onwards towards
the coveted goal of their most ardent wishes.

But some of the new arrivals stayed behind in
Victoria to make more certain fortunes looking after the
needs of the miners. Within a six-week period, no less
than two hundred and twenty-five new buildings went
up, nearly two hundred of them stores. Land values
skyrocketed from between $50 and $75 for a good town
lot to between $1,500 and $3,000 and even higher.

Douglas had little time to eat or sleep that spring
and summer. He knew it was physically impossible to
stop the tide of gold-seekers, but he was determined
not to lose control of the situation.

The two most immediate fears he had were a

takeover by the United States and a repeat of the violence and lawlessness that had dominated the California gold rush ten years earlier. As Governor of Vancouver Island, he knew he had no legal authority at all on the Mainland, but as Chief Factor of the Hudson's Bay Company (which did have some legal rights there) he acted swiftly to take control until he could get instructions from the British government.

What methods did the miners use to collect the gold? Were they able to work all through the year? What were the living conditions like in the gold fields?

With a mere handful of soldiers and officials, he had little means of enforcing the rule of British law and institutions on the newcomers, but he and his men were all good bluffers. Setting out on the Hudson's Bay ship, *Otter*, they crossed the straits to visit the gold fields and see first-hand what was happening there. Along the way, Douglas appointed revenue officers to collect licence fees from the miners as well as justices of the peace and a small police force to keep law and order.

Several clashes between the prospectors and the Indian tribes living on the river had already taken place by the time the Governor arrived. The native people were as alarmed as he was by the sudden arrival of these unruly newcomers. At each stop that Douglas made, he warned the miners that the Indians had the same rights and privileges under British law as they did, but many of them did not believe this.

They brought with them terrible tales of how the native people in the United States were being herded onto reservations. The Governor had to work very hard to convince the Fraser River tribes that this would not happen to them. He also guaranteed their hunting and fishing rights in the area and instructed his new law officers to see that his promises were carried out. As long as he remained the Queen's representative on the Pacific Coast, Douglas was true to his word.

When the Governor returned to Victoria, he decided that more safe boats must be made available to transport the miners to the gold fields. He gave permission for several American steamers to operate on the Fraser and even put the *Beaver* and the *Otter* on the run from Victoria to the Mainland to keep down passenger and freight prices.

Loaded with men and supplies, the American sternwheeler, *Umatilla*, was the first large boat to reach Fort Yale. Struggling against a treacherous current, she

took five hours to travel the twenty-five kilometres from Fort Hope to Yale cheered on by the miners, shouting their encouragement from the river bank and shooting their guns and pistols into the air. On the return journey, she slipped down the river in fifty-one minutes like "a streak of chain lightning!"

In spite of his administrative worries, the Governor also caught the gold fever. He was soon writing enthusiastically to the Colonial Secretary, "the whole country situated to the eastward of the Gulf of Georgia, as far north as Johnstone's Straits, is one continued bed of gold of incalculable value and extent."

Months passed between Douglas' urgent dispatches sent half way around the world to London and the replies that eventually made their way back to him. During that time he had taken complete management of affairs into his own hands and made all necessary decisions about mining regulations, policing, road building and trade.

Finally he learned that the British government looked favourably on the strong control he had managed to gain over the explosive situation. There was only one thing wrong, and the Colonial Secretary told him so in very blunt terms.

Sternwheelers soon began taking hundreds of miners up the Fraser River to Fort Yale. These ships could float in less than a metre of water and needed no landing docks. The captain could run the ship up on the shore and throw out a plank. To get back into mid-stream he only had to reverse the stern paddles.

The Hudson's Bay Company have hitherto had an exclusive right to trade with Indians in the Fraser's River Territory, but they have had no other right whatever. They have had no right to exclude strangers. They have had no rights of Government, or of occupation of the soil. They have had no right to prevent or interfere with any kind of trading, except with Indians alone.

Now, he informed Douglas, the Company would lose even those rights because Her Majesty's government had decided to establish a Crown colony on the Mainland, henceforward to be called British Columbia.

Much of the sting of the Colonial Secretary's words disappeared when, in the next sentence, he offered Douglas an appointment as governor of the new "gold colony." But he made one condition. Douglas would have to give up all connection with the company he had served for thirty-seven years.

On October 4, 1858 the old fur trader resigned from the commercial empire of the Hudson's Bay Company to become the governor of not one but two Crown colonies.

Judge Begbie took James Douglas's oath of allegiance to the Queen in the ceremony creating the province of British Columbia.

Breathing Chapter 10
Space

For nearly six months Governor Douglas had been almost alone fighting to protect Britain's possessions on the Pacific Coast. Now help was on the way as other men with a wide variety of talents made their way across the oceans of the world to join him.

First to arrive from patrol in the Orient was Rear Admiral Robert Baynes, commanding one of the most impressive sailing battleships of the day. The *Ganges* mounted eighty-four guns on three decks, and could safely transport eight hundred men. The security of the West Coast was much less in doubt after Admiral Baynes arrived.

Next came a detachment of the Royal Engineers, a small force of military specialists under the command of Colonel Richard Moody. The engineers would prove extremely useful in opening up the gold colony's land communications, but their first task was to pick a site for a capital city on the Mainland. Colonel Moody and his men chose a quiet spot on the banks of the Fraser River and there mapped out the future townsite of New Westminster.

Certainly the most colourful figure dispatched by the British government at this time was Matthew Baillie Begbie, the first judge for the colony. Like Douglas, he was a man of tremendous stamina with a strong belief in law and order. Always dressed in his flowing black judge's robes, he soon became famous for his exhausting travels on horseback through the sprawling gold fields which served as his courthouse.

Backing up Judge Begbie was a plucky Irishman, Chartres Brew, who had served fourteen years in the Irish Constabulary before being sent to British Columbia to organize a small police force. As Inspector of Police for the gold colony, he was not above

Colonel Richard Clement Moody of the Royal Engineers

Begbie was known as "the Hanging Judge." Why? Was the nickname justified?

Amor De Cosmos' real name was William Smith. Why did he change his name? What does it mean?

After British Columbia joined Confederation in 1871, De Cosmos was elected Premier of the new province. Following that he became a federal Member of Parliament for eight years and died insane at the age of seventy-two. What was the fate of his counterpart, John Robson?

personally knocking heads together when the miners got out of hand.

Over the next few years, the Governor relied heavily on the judgement and good advice of these men. But he was not so happy with some of the other new arrivals who swept in on the coattails of the Fraser River gold rush.

From the moment they set foot on West Coast soil, Amor De Cosmos and John Robson became the Governor's toughest critics. De Cosmos was a Nova Scotian who had spent some years as a photographer in California before moving north to establish Victoria's first newspaper, the *British Colonist*. Robson came from Upper Canada a year later to set up the Mainland's first newspaper, the *British Columbian*.

From the day the first editions rolled off the press, both men turned their editorial pens on Douglas. Although their writing sometimes bordered on the hysterical and often degenerated into personal insults, they collected enough popular support and sympathy to make his political life very uncomfortable.

Both editors accused him of obstructing the introduction of representative government in the colonies. Douglas never tried to deny this; he simply did not believe in democratic institutions. Working as he had for the Hudson's Bay Company, he had learned that the word of a senior official was as good as law and not open to question except from those above him. Transferring this rule to colonial government, he could see no more logic in local government participation than in a Company *voyageur* or clerk trying to tell a Chief Factor how to run his department. What would have happened if he had waited around while everyone discussed how to handle the gold rush? They would probably still be arguing about what to do. When he wanted advice, he always asked for it, but in the end he preferred the decision — and the responsibility — to rest with him alone.

But time was against him. On direct orders from England, he had to introduce representative government to both colonies before he retired from office.

Douglas did not spend much time brooding over his critics. That had never been his way. Now that Begbie,

Moody and the others were handling some of the
day-to-day decisions on the Mainland, he was able to
give closer attention to what was happening in Victoria
and, hopefully, spend a little more time with his family.

The Island's capital was growing fast. Social
activities had become very lively indeed with concerts
and dinner parties and dances every week. On official
holidays, Governor Douglas was busy receiving callers
and attending special events, such as horse races in
Beacon Hill Park. He was always accompanied by one
or two of his daughters who enjoyed these outings
almost as much as he did.

Although Douglas was deeply attached to his wife,
he never insisted that she perform any of the social
duties normally expected of a Governor's wife. When
Amelia Douglas did receive visitors at the Governor's
home, they always remarked on her gentle and kindly
manner, but she was still very shy and self-conscious
about the way she spoke English. The usual language of
the Douglas household was either Indian or French
Canadian.

*By the end of 1858, people of
many different races had made
Victoria their home. What were
some of the larger groups and
why did each of them settle
there?*

*The south front of James
Douglas's home at 603 Superior
Street, Victoria. Amelia
Douglas and her brother are on
the Veranda.*

Besides, Amelia still had two young children to look after. James, the only son in the family, was a sickly child of nine who required constant care, and Martha, the youngest, was not yet six. The older girls did not mind at all if their mother left the social responsibilities to them, and the Governor soon became accustomed to this arrangement.

Everyone in Victoria welcomed the gold rush money which continued to pour in, but few people were happy with the haphazard way the town had sprouted. It was no longer the crowded tent city of the spring, but the streets had become so boggy that signs appeared everywhere warning "no bottom obtainable" or "two men in this hole!" Horses, cows and pigs wandered the streets at will, and open sewers ran alongside newly constructed boardwalks. Douglas commented to a friend, "This city suffers from an excess of politicians, lawyers, merchants, transients and saloons and a considerable shortage of accommodation, water, women and good roads!"

A view of Yates Street, Victoria, in 1862, from the corner of Government and Wharf Streets. Many of the people shown in this sketch are Chinese immigrants or Indians.

But luckily there was plenty of money around and he lost no time in siphoning off as much as he

could to improve the situation. New public buildings
sprang up, streets were paved and construction of the
first legislative buildings got under way. Citizens
soon nicknamed the new seat of government, "The
Birdcages," and the local press described the buildings
as "something between a Dutch toy and a Chinese
pagoda."

But Victoria had moved rapidly from a sleepy
trading village to a booming coastal city, and everyone,
including the Governor, was proud of it.

*Top: The old legislative
buildings in Victoria, built in
1860 and nicknamed "The
Birdcages"*

*Bottom: Government Street,
Victoria, in the early 1860s. The
usual method of supplying
water before water mains were
built was by horse-drawn water
barrels.*

Chapter 11 The San Juan Pig

Admiral Baynes thumped his fist on the table.

"It is ridiculous to go to war over the shooting of a pig!" he declared.

"If that were the sum total of this affair, sir, I would agree with you completely," replied the Governor coolly. "But as I have told you already, I believe it is more serious than that. American troops should not be permitted to remain on San Juan Island while we stand by watching. They'll be in Victoria next!

"When all those American miners and sympathizers on the Mainland hear that we've done nothing, it won't be long before they make a move too. You should hear some of the songs they're singing."

The Governor had heard many of these songs on his trips to the gold fields and New Westminster. He remembered one verse especially:

Soon our banner will be streaming,
Soon the eagle will be screaming,
And the lion—see it cowers,
Hurrah, boys, the river's ours.

Admiral Baynes rose slowly and said, "I will not order a naval attack on San Juan. Such an action could spark a war between Britain and the United States, and I am not at all sure that is what Her Majesty's government has in mind. I have asked for instructions from London and I intend to wait until I receive them."

"The Pig Episode" all began on the small island of San Juan situated in the straits between Victoria and the American mainland. Both Britain and the United States had claims to the island, but while discussions continued between the two governments, the Hudson's Bay Company still maintained a sheep farm there and a number of American settlers had moved in.

One day in the summer of 1859, a settler got so

angry with a huge Company pig for rooting up his
potatoes that he shot the animal. The British,
represented by the Crown colony of Vancouver Island,
insisted that the settler pay $100 for the dead pig or
come to Victoria to stand trial. He refused to do either,
and was soon backed up by a contingent of troops from
the American mainland. They had stationed themselves
on the island to "protect American settlers from Indians
and the Hudson's Bay Company," and refused to allow
any British troops to land on San Juan.

American soldiers on San Juan

Douglas was furious. Knowing that the British forces on the Pacific Coast were much stronger than the American, he wanted to act immediately to drive the American forces off the island. British land and sea forces were readied for the fight, but the Governor's Legislative Council and Admiral Baynes were strongly against taking action. They preferred negotiation to war and, in the end, they proved to be right, at least in the short run.

When word reached London and Washington, both governments were relieved that they had so narrowly missed going to war. President Lincoln severely reprimanded the American general who had ordered troops onto the island for his "ill-considered and hasty action," and quickly approved a joint occupation of San Juan by a small force of British and American soldiers. The question of payment for the pig was forgotten in the commotion and diplomatic negotiations.

Another twelve years went by and the two countries had still not made up their minds who should have the island. Finally they asked the German Emperor to decide for them, promising to abide by his ruling in the matter. In 1872 he awarded the island of San Juan and several other islands around it to the United States.

Why was President Lincoln so anxious to avoid a war with Britain at this time?

The Great Roads
Chapter 12

On his two visits to the gold fields in the summer of 1858, the Governor had soon realized that the search for the precious metal would not stop at Fort Yale. With the quantities of gold now being collected on the lower Fraser River, most miners were willing to wager everything they had that more of the same would be found further upstream.

Douglas listened with fascination as the miners related hair-raising tales of their attempts to conquer the narrow gorges of the canyon above Fort Yale. Some had tried building canoes and rafts to break through the treacherous rapids and whirlpools. When that had failed, they had taken to the narrow Indian trails cut into the canyon face. Many had already lost valuable tools and supplies paid for with their life savings, but at least they had escaped with their lives. Others had not been so lucky.

Douglas recalled Simon Fraser's description of the area when he had explored the river fifty years earlier. "I cannot find words to describe our situation at times," he had written. "We have to pass where no human being should venture." An alternative would have to be found.

It was not long before the Governor was laying plans for the construction of an easier, if considerably longer, route to the upper Fraser River using a chain of lakes lying between the Harrison River and the settlement of Lillooet.

When the miners heard about his scheme, five hundred of them volunteered to help build the road as well as the boats needed to cross the four lakes on the route. Douglas jumped at the offer, agreeing to transport the men and give them room and board in exchange for their free labour. Each miner had to

A mule train going over the mountain passes before the Cariboo Road was built

"To the Diggings and from the Diggings"

deposit $25 with the Governor as a guarantee of good behaviour.

In August 1858 the sternwheeler, *Umatilla*, transported the volunteers and supplies to the head of Harrison Lake. The men were ready to begin work immediately, but not before giving three hearty cheers for the Governor and three more for the supervisor of the project, Alexander Anderson. They named the starting point of their road Port Douglas.

Everyone worked as though possessed by the devil, always with the dream of gold glittering before his eyes. By the end of the year, the one hundred and seventy kilometre Harrison-Lillooet Road was open to traffic, and miners began streaming over it into the heartland of British Columbia.

Douglas reported proudly to his superiors in London that the project had cost only £14,000, but they were not impressed. As far as Britain was concerned all colonies, no matter what their size or circumstances, should be completely self-supporting. In this regard British Columbia was not the ideal colony in spite of Douglas's reassurances that great financial benefits were only just around the corner.

Two years later the Harrison-Lillooet Road had been expanded into an impressive four-metre-wide wagon road, but the journey was still a long and tedious one. Supplies had to be loaded on and off boats eight times to cross the lakes between Port Douglas and Lillooet.

Late in 1860 the first major gold strike was reported from a remote valley in the Cariboo at a place called Keithley Creek. With this encouraging news, prospectors pushed further and further into the interior in search of the illusive mother lode.

Soon deposits far richer than any ever found on the lower Fraser River were discovered at Antler Creek, bringing a new wave of miners flooding into the country. There was really only one thing to discourage them: the higher and higher cost of transport for themselves and their supplies as they moved away from the Coast.

But gold is like a strong magnet, and Douglas knew that the miners would get there no matter what the obstacles. His main objective was to control the human tide as best he could and preferably collect some

Working a gold mining dump box at the Ne'er Do Well claim at Grouse Creek

revenue from it to pay for public works in the colony. He had built the Harrison-Lillooet Road for that reason and it had served the colony well. But unfortunately it was not good enough to handle the new situation.

Many Americans were pressing hard for another road, but the Governor did not like the proposed route at all. Many of the miners had come through the Oregon Territory, crossing the border near the Okanagan lakes and travelling north on the old fur brigade trail. But in Douglas's eyes, developing such a route was like handling dynamite. It could eventually divert the whole trade of the interior into American hands and probably the Crown colony of British Columbia as well. Even the idea was intolerable! He really had only one alternative. The Fraser Canyon was the most direct route from the Coast to the Cariboo. Any new road would have to go through it.

Douglas was soon poring over plans and maps with Colonel Moody who was to supervise the whole project. Most of the proposed road was divided into sections and assigned to private contractors in an attempt to get the road built as quickly as possible. But two sections, between Yale and Boston Bar and

Trace the routes of the Harrison-Lillooet Road and the Cariboo Road on a map. How long were they used?

around Cook's Ferry, would need the special skills of Colonel Moody and the Royal Engineers.

The next problem was how to raise money to pay the contractors. Douglas recognized the difficulty but decided the important thing was to get the road started. Financial details could be worked out later.

Work on the Cariboo Road began almost immediately, just as Douglas had promised. He drew up a separate agreement for each section of road allowing the contractor to charge a toll for five or six years on everything that passed through to cover part of his costs.

Where the plan called for the route to cross the mighty Fraser, ingenious bridges had to be designed and thrown across the canyon. One suspension bridge at Spuzzum, the Alexandra Bridge, was nearly one hundred metres long. Proclaimed as an engineering marvel, it was so well built that a heavily loaded wagon could cross it without danger.

Other parts of the road had to be blasted from the sides of rocky gorges or built on trestles over the raging waters below.

Why is this called a suspension bridge? Where and when were some other famous suspension bridges built?

It was nearly six months before Douglas could leave his duties on the Coast to make a personal inspection of the road construction. He was delighted with everything he saw and reported the progress to the Colonial Secretary.

I cannot speak too favourably of the newly formed roads. In smoothness and solidity they surpass expectation—Jackass Mountain, the Cleft, the Great Slides, the Rocky Bridges, and other passes of ominous fame, so notorious in the history of the country, have lost their former terrors.

But not everyone was as enthusiastic about his wonderful new road. A year later the first tourists to cross the Rocky Mountains from Eastern Canada, Lord Milton and Dr. Cheadle, pronounced it "the most dangerous carriage road I ever saw." Travelling by express wagon, they were particularly alarmed by one section descending Pavillion Mountain:

The road turns six times, is very narrow except at the turns, the mountainside terrifically steep. We rattled down at a fearful pace—a wheel coming off, the brake giving way, or a restive horse, being almost certain death.

The Cariboo Road went through Hell's Gate Canyon on the Fraser River

A mule train on the Cariboo Road at Great Bluff above the Thompson River, about 140 km above Yale

"A Wayside House at Midnight"

How did Douglas finance the building of the Cariboo Road? How much did it cost in the end?

Why were camels brought to British Columbia during the Cariboo gold rush? What happened to them afterwards?

The great Cariboo Road was not completely finished until 1865, a year after Governor Douglas retired. But it was in heavy use long before that. It ran from Fort Yale nearly six hundred and fifty kilometres to Barkerville in the heart of the gold fields.

In its heyday thousands of miners on foot, great covered wagons, pack trains of up to sixty animals, stage coaches and even camels travelled the road. Roadhouses sprang up every fifteen or twenty-five kilometres to provide food and lodging for travellers and fresh horses for the stage coaches. If a traveller was strong enough to stand the pace, he could get from Yale to Barkerville in four days.

In just one year, six and a half million dollars worth of gold was shipped along the new road to the Coast. Once and for all, the Governor had succeeded in binding the fantastic wealth of the British Columbia interior to the centres of economic activity on the Coast. But perhaps more important in the long run, the whole interior was now open to settlement and commerce on a broad scale.

The wild, isolated territory that James Douglas had first known thirty years before as New Caledonia would never be the same again.

"A Pyramid of Gold and Gems"

Chapter 13

James Douglas moved slowly up the gangplank with Amelia on his arm. When they reached the top, he guided his wife to the ship's rail as guns boomed out a salute and the crowd of well-wishers sang "For he's a jolly good fellow."

The cheers and shouts of "Good luck, Sir James!" rang in his ears as the *Enterprise* pulled away from the wharf. Yes, indeed, Sir James Douglas, K.C.B. It did have a rather pleasant ring to it, he thought. From the way the citizens of Victoria were behaving, one would think that the Queen had bestowed a title on the whole city.

A few days earlier he had made his official farewells as Governor of Vancouver Island at an elaborate banquet given in his honour. Now he was crossing the Strait of Georgia to hand over his Mainland responsibilities to the newly appointed Governor for British Columbia.

It was just as well that Her Majesty had decided to divide his duties between two men, he thought to himself. The colonies were growing so rapidly and had such different problems that a man would have to be a magician to look after both of them. Perhaps that was what he had been all these years—a magician.

Who succeeded Douglas as Governor in each of the colonies? What policies did they have that were different from his?

Not to be outdone by the Vancouver Islanders, the people of British Columbia were planning a banquet of their own at the Mainland's capital city. Of course, it would not be as big or lavish as the first one had been, but then no one would expect it to be.

New Westminster was just five years old with a population numbering in the hundreds. By

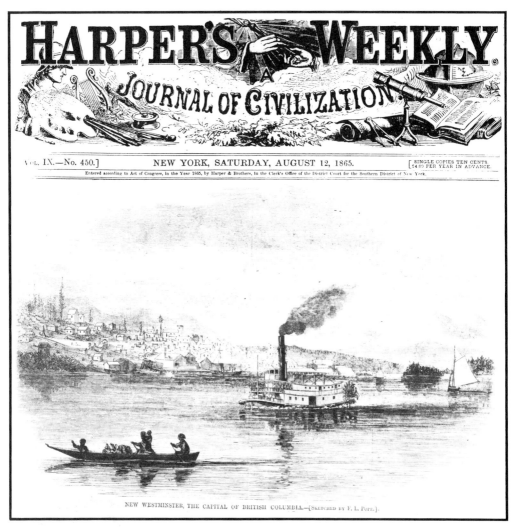

HARPER'S WEEKLY.

A JOURNAL OF CIVILIZATION.

Vol. IX.—No. 450.]   NEW YORK, SATURDAY, AUGUST 12, 1865.   [SINGLE COPIES TEN CENTS.
$4.00 PER YEAR IN ADVANCE.

Entered according to Act of Congress, in the Year 1865, by Harper & Brothers, in the Clerk's Office of the District Court for the Southern District of New York.

NEW WESTMINSTER, THE CAPITAL OF BRITISH COLUMBIA.—[Sketched by F. L. Pope.]

New Westminster as Douglas would have seen it when he retired as Governor of the colony

comparison, Victoria was a major metropolis with a population of 6,000, paved streets, and gas and water piped to most establishments. But even though New Westminster was nicknamed "the city of stumps," it did have one thing that Victoria would find hard to beat: a magnificent main street thirty-three metres wide laid out by Colonel Moody when he first planned the city.

The banquet was delicious and served in a most gracious manner. Then it was time for the speeches. Sir James gave his wife a quick smile of reassurance; he was deeply touched that she had overcome her usual shyness and agreed to accompany him on the last of his official duties.

Attorney-General Crease rose, and holding a beautifully illuminated paper, explained that it had been signed by more than nine hundred people from all over the colony and sent to the British government in London as a memorial to the Governor's achievements. It emphasized his great road system, his concern for equal justice and the rule of law, and his tireless devotion to the heavy duties of his offices. His work had not gone unnoticed.

When the Attorney-General presented him with a copy of the address, Sir James examined it quietly while the applause swirled around him. Then he rose slowly from his chair and began to speak.

"A pyramid of gold and gems would have been less acceptable to me than this simple record. I ask for no prouder monument, and for no other memorial, when I die and go hence, than the testimony here offered, that I have done my duty."

To bid everyone farewell as Governor was more difficult than he had imagined, but he had no regrets about greeting them again as a private citizen. At sixty years old, he looked forward to spending more time with his family, attending to his own business affairs and travelling abroad.

Within a month of his retirement, Sir James set out to accomplish at least one of these goals. On May 14, 1864 he kissed Amelia and little Martha goodbye and boarded the *Sierra Nevada* for his first voyage on a steam-powered ocean liner. It was nearly half a century since he had returned to his homeland, and he did not intend to delay the pilgrimage any longer.

The plaque of Douglas by James Syme, presented to Lady Douglas when her husband retired as Governor of the Mainland colony in 1864

First he visited friends and relatives in England and Scotland. He took particular pleasure in a reunion with his daughter, Jane, whose husband had succeeded Sir George Simpson as Governor of the Hudson's Bay Company operations in North America, and with his son, James, who was attending school in England.

But he spent most of his time, nearly eight months, travelling on the Continent where he toured almost every country. Exactly one year after his departure, Douglas returned home to Victoria.

The Father of British Columbia Chapter 14

Sir James enjoyed his retirement almost as much as he had enjoyed directing the affairs of Vancouver Island and British Columbia.

Remaining in good health until the day he died, he rose every morning at six, bathed, said his prayers and went for a ride through the neighbourhood before sitting down to breakfast at the stroke of nine. As the largest landowner in Victoria, he had to spend some time each month managing his properties, but most of his day he preferred to devote to his family and friends.

Sir James was happiest when he was surrounded by his many grandchildren, taking them to the beach or on long drives and picnics in the country whenever he could. "Having been a wanderer . . . for more than forty years," he wrote to a relative in Paris, "I enjoy with the keenest relish the quiet pleasures of my own fireside."

After his retirement, Sir James took no part in politics, but from his private letters it is obvious that he watched with the keenest interest the progress of the two colonies he had founded. He saw them united under the name of British Columbia with his beloved Victoria chosen as the capital city. And in 1871 he saw the colony enter Confederation with the promise of a great railway to bind the East and West of British North America firmly together.

When he died on August 2, 1877 at the age of 74, Sir James Douglas's place in history was assured. Thousands of people gathered in Victoria to pay their last respects at the largest and most elaborate funeral ever held in that city, then or since. The *Victoria Colonist* published a final tribute on behalf of them all:

When were the colonies of Victoria and British Columbia united? Why? Who became the first governor of the united colony?

Lady Douglas after Sir James's death

Wax likeness of Sir James Douglas

No history of the province can be written without Sir James Douglas forming the central figure around which will cluster the stirring events that have marked the advance of the province from a fur-hunting preserve for nomadic tribes to a progressive country of civilized beings under the protection of the British flag and enjoying a stable and settled form of government . . .

Truly, he has set an example of goodness and patriotism worthy of being copied by future generations of British Columbians.

It was a fine dedication to a man who had earned it, but perhaps he would have appreciated most of all the simple tribute offered by his old friend, Bishop Cridge: "The right man was in the right place."

The funeral procession for Sir James Douglas, August 6, 1877

The Pacific Northwest
1825-1865

Fort Taku

Sitka

Fort Stikine

Boundary of present province of British Columbia

Fort
St. James

Barkerville

Keithley Creek

Fort
Alexandria

Fraser River

CARIBOO COUNTRY

Columbia River

Lillooet

Pavillion
Mountain

Fort Kamloops

Port Douglas
Boston Bar
Spuzzum
Lake
Okanagan

Harrison
Lake

Fort Yale

VANCOUVER ISLAND

Strait of Georgia

Fort Hope

49°

Strait of Juan de Fuca

Nanaimo

New
Westminster

Fort
Victoria

San Juan Islands

Fort Nisqually

0   100   200   300

Kilometres

Fort Vancouver

Further Reading

Downs, Art. *Paddlewheels on the Frontier*. Sidney, B.C.: Gray's Publishing, 1972.

Innis, Harold A. *The Fur Trade in Canada*. Toronto: University of Toronto Press, 1930.

MacKay, Douglas. *The Honourable Company: A History of the Hudson's Bay Company*. Toronto: McClelland and Stewart, 1936.

Neering, Rosemary, *Fur Trade*. Toronto: Fitzhenry and Whiteside, 1974.

Ormsby, Margaret A. *British Columbia: A History*. Toronto: MacMillan, 1958.

Pethick, Derek. *James Douglas: Servant of Two Empires*. Vancouver: Mitchell Press, 1969.

_____ . *S.S. Beaver: The Ship That Saved the West*. Vancouver: Mitchell Press, 1970.

Place, Marian T. *Cariboo Gold: The Story of the British Columbia Gold Rush*. New York: Holt, Rinehart and Winston, 1970.

Smith, Dorothy Blakey. *James Douglas: Father of British Columbia*. Toronto: Oxford University Press, 1971.

Credits

The author wishes to thank the following for their help: The British Columbia Provincial Archives, in particular the Photographic Section, and The City of Vancouver Archives.

The publishers wish to express their gratitude to the following who have given permission to use copyrighted illustrations in this book:
City Archives, Vancouver, B.C., page 56
Courtesy of the American Museum of Natural History, page 5
Hudson's Bay Company, pages 3, 9, 11, 25
Minnesota Historical Society, *Aspects of the Fur Trade*, pages 4, 7, 10
Newberry Library, Chicago, page 6
New York Public Library, page 2
Oblate Society of Manitoba, pages 8, 15
Provincial Archives, Victoria, B.C., pages 12, 17, 18, 19, 20, 21, 24, 27, 28, 29, 30, 31, 34, 36, 37, 39, 40, 41, 42, 43, 44, 45, 47, 49, 50, 51, 52, 53, 54, 57, 58, 59, 60
Robert Banks, page 40
Royal London Wax Museum, Victoria, B.C., page 60

Editing: Heather Sherratt
Design: Jack Steiner
Cover Illustration: Peter Sit

The Canadians

Consulting Editor: Roderick Stewart
Editor-in-Chief: Robert Read

Every effort has been made to credit all sources correctly. The author and publishers will welcome any information that will allow them to correct any errors or omissions.